W9-BAZ-941

Peyton Manning

Riddell
18

Peyton Manning

Michael Bradley

BENCHMARK BOOKS

MARSHALL CAVENDISH
NEW YORK

Benchmark Books
Marshall Cavendish
99 White Plains Road
Tarrytown, NY 10591-9001
www.marshallcavendish.com

Library of Congress Cataloging-in-Publication Data

Bradley, Michael, 1962-
Peyton Manning / Michael Bradley.
p. cm.—(Benchmark all-stars)
Summary: Discusses the personal life and football career of the Indianapolis Colts quarterback.
Includes bibliographical references and index.
ISBN 0-7614-1628-5
1. Manning, Peyton—Juvenile literature. 2. Football players—United States—Biography—Juvenile literature. [1. Manning, Peyton. 2. Football players.] I. Title. II. Series.

GV939.M289B73 2003
796.332'092--dc21

2003001450

Photo research by Regina Flanagan.
Cover: AP/Wide World Photos
AFP/*Corbis*: 6, 43; Damian Strohmeyer/Sports Illustrated (top); John McDonough/Sports Illustrated (bottom): 8; Al Tielemans/Sports Illustrated: 2–3, 9, 20; Reuters NewMedia/*Corbis*: 10, 41, 42, 44; AP/Wide World Photos: 11, 32, 34, 35, 38, 40; Icon Sports Media: 12; Lane Stewart/Sports Illustrated: 14; Bill Frakes/Sports Illustrated: 15, 16, 21, 26, 27; Bill Frakes/Sports Illustrated (top): 17; Patrick Murphy-Racey/Sports Illustrated (bottom): 17; Damian Strohmeyer/Sports Illustrated: 18, 24, 30; Robert Rogers/Sports Illustrated: 22, 23; John Biever: 28; John Iacono/Sports Illustrated: 29; Thomas B. Shea/Icon Sports Media: 36; Dave Kaup/AFP Photo: 39.

Series design by Becky Terhune
Printed in Italy
1 3 5 6 4 2

Contents

Peyton Manning gets ready to throw.

CHAPTER ONE

Trying to Be the Best

Peyton Manning doesn't know how to cook. He has trouble with directions. He needs snapshots of color-coordinated outfits to help him get dressed. But on a football field, he can do it all. There, he doesn't worry about how the microwave works or whether a black jacket goes with brown pants. He is so prepared, so ready to play, and so talented that it all comes together. Perfectly.

On October 31, 1999, in his second year with the National Football League, Manning and the Indianapolis Colts faced the Dallas Cowboys. As the fourth quarter began, the teams were tied at 24–24, and the Colts had the ball on the Dallas 40-yard line. It was time for some of that Manning magic. He took the *snap* and made a perfect *fake* to running back Edgerrin James. Dallas cornerback Deion "Prime Time" Sanders was completely fooled and Colts receiver Marvin Harrison was able to dash behind him. Manning hit Harrison with a perfect strike for a *touchdown*.

Later, with the Colts holding on to a 31–24 lead and facing a third *down* deep in their own territory, Manning struck again. This time, he scrambled from the pocket and found James alone near the sideline. The *quarterback* ran 54 yards (49 m) to set up a field goal that clinched the victory for the Colts.

Peyton Manning hands off the ball to an Indianapolis teammate, starting another successful Colts play.

Two big plays. Two examples of Peyton Manning's skill. More importantly, they are two examples of how prepared the Colts quarterback is. The great fake to James on the touchdown pass came from hours of studying film of other quarterbacks' *technique*. The pass to James was a by-product of a drill Manning learned from his father—former pro-football passing great Archie Manning.

For some people, quarterbacking is all about a strong arm. For Manning, it's about everything. No player in the NFL spends more time trying to improve. No player watches more game tape. Nobody practices harder. He even takes some plays on the kickoff team, the unit that covers kickoffs to opponents, just to give his teammates a rest. The NFL has had plenty of great quarterbacks in its history, and many believe that Peyton Manning will join the list when his career is over.

Ready to deliver: Manning is poised and efficient in the pocket—two big reasons for his success.

Manning has all the physical tools, but it

From stretching to watching films, few quarterbacks do as much to prepare as Peyton Manning does.

is his desire and willingness to improve that set him apart. Ever since he started his first game as a high school sophomore, Manning has been devoted to becoming the best quarterback out there. It won't be long until he reaches his goal.

"He's easily one of the top ten quarterbacks in football, and that's a conservative statement, because there aren't nine guys I'd put ahead of him," *Monday Night Football* analyst John Madden said in 1999. "I always had the theory that a quarterback doesn't have a clue until his fifth year, but with this guy, that goes right out the window."

Manning isn't a speedster, but he has the strength to elude oncoming defenders.

Since joining the Colts in 1998 after a fabulous career at the University of Tennessee, Manning has helped the team move from last place to perennial play-off contender. He has done it with a commitment that is unmatched. And even though some of his teammates tease him about not knowing a frying pan from a wok or how to find some of his favorite restaurants by car, they can't find fault with Manning as a teammate. His difficulties with life's daily tasks off the field are a direct by-product of his devotion to life on it. Who has time to learn how to cook when there are game tapes to watch? Laundry? No way. He would rather go lift some weights or run some sprints.

When he joined the Colts, Peyton Manning asked to have his locker located with the offensive linemen since they would have to protect him from enemy pass rushers. No superstar ego here. As a junior at Tennessee, he was invited to attend the banquet honoring college football's best quarterback. Even though Manning knew he hadn't won, he went anyway, just to talk with some of the other great passers who would be there.

"He's easily one of the top ten quarterbacks in football, and that's a conservative statement, because there aren't nine guys I'd put ahead of him."
—John Madden

"I figured I had two hours with those guys," Manning said. "I wasn't going to waste it by making small talk." Nobody would blame him if he acted like a star. After all, he's the son of Archie Manning, who is considered one of the greatest college quarterbacks of all time. Archie Manning was a legend at the University of Mississippi, and was an extremely popular player with the New Orleans Saints. But Peyton Manning didn't consider himself all that special, even when he was thrilling University of Tennessee fans by setting thirty-three different school records. He's just your everyday, average guy—who happens to be a *Pro Bowl* quarterback.

No quarterback in University of Mississippi history was as talented or beloved as Archie Manning.

"The great thing about Peyton is he comes across as being very mortal," says Bill Musgrave, who roomed with Manning during training camp in 1988. "The only other person at that level I've seen who can convey that was John Elway. He and Peyton are both tremendous athletes who don't carry themselves like they're superhuman."

Even though they may appear that way on the field.

Archie Manning with the ball.

CHAPTER TWO

Great Bloodlines

After New Orleans Saints games, Peyton Manning and his older brother, Cooper, would make footballs out of used athletic tape and play on the turf at the Louisiana Superdome. Could there be anything more perfect for two boys? The Manning brothers would watch the New Orleans Saints from the stands with their mother, Olivia, and then head to the locker room. There they would watch their father get changed and talk to reporters, usually about another Saints loss. Throughout Archie Manning's career in New Orleans, from 1971 to 1981, the Saints had 44 wins, 115 losses, and 3 decisions. They never had a winning season, and in 1980 finished 1 and 15. After the locker room, it was onto the field. Peyton and Cooper would pretend they were NFL stars. They would play pitch-and-catch. They would run and tackle. And then they would fight. Their father would always have to break it up.

"The day you two can finish a game without a fight will be a great day in my life," Archie Manning would tell his sons. That was how it was growing up the son of an NFL star. Free tickets to games. Hanging out in locker rooms. Playing in the Superdome. Growing up just a couple of blocks from the Mardi Gras parade route in a big, beautiful

A family affair: Archie Manning poses with his wife, Olivia, and sons (L-R) Eli, Peyton, and Cooper.

southern house. The Manning boys knew their dad was something special. They could tell by the cheers—and, occasionally, the boos. But they didn't know he was practically college football royalty. Archie Manning had led the University of Mississippi to the 1970 Sugar Bowl. He finished third in the 1970 *Heisman Trophy* balloting. And when the Rebels chose their all-century team, asymbolic collection of the best players who played at the school from 1900 to 1999, he was quarterback.

Even though Archie Manning didn't push his children into football, they couldn't help but play it. Cooper, who is two years older than Peyton, was the star receiver. He was laid-back and carefree, able to make people laugh. Peyton was much more intense, even as a young boy. He had to do everything right. He worried about the details. No wonder they fought. The two boys were as different as could be.

"I think my dad was glad I was around to keep Peyton from having a heart attack in fourth grade when his science project was late," Cooper Manning once said.

No one really knew just how well Peyton could play until his sophomore year at New Orleans's Isidore Newman High School when he earned the starting-quarterback job. That was a magical season for the Mannings. Cooper caught 80 passes—all from his little

Manning's Isidore Newman High School career was filled with success and acclaim.

brother. Newman went 12 and 2 and made it to the state semifinals. "It was just like playing in the backyard," Peyton said. It was, except the two brothers were now friends and teammates, not rivals.

"That year made us buddies," Cooper said. Everybody expected the Manning brothers to continue their pitch-and-catch show at the University of Mississippi, especially when Cooper signed a letter of intent to play there in 1992.

It never happened. Cooper had played half of his senior high school season with numbness in his right hand. After one game in his freshman year at Mississippi, he reported that his right leg was numb.

Archie Manning

Few players in college football history have captured the imagination of a school and a nation the way Elisha Archibald Manning did during his time at the University of Mississippi. From the moment he moved into the starting lineup as quarterback, during the 1968 season, Manning was a true phenomenon.

He led the Rebels to a 22–10–1 record during his three years as a starter, but his contribution to the program was measured not only in wins and losses, but also in sheer excitement. The redheaded quarterback was a dynamic passer and a dangerous runner, who could torment a team's defenses in many different ways. A prime example of his overwhelming skills came in a thrilling—though heartbreaking for Mississippi fans—33–32 loss to Alabama in 1969. In that game, Manning threw for 436 yards (399 m) and rushed for another 104 (95 m).

Manning led the Rebels to three bowl games and helped Mississippi win two of them—the 1968 Liberty Bowl, over Virginia Tech, and the 1970 Sugar Bowl, over Arkansas.

Even as a high schooler, Peyton displayed the skills and drive that made him one of the NFL's best.

After numerous tests and consultations, the Mannings learned that their oldest son had spinal stenosis, a narrowing of the spinal cavity. One more hit from the wrong direction, at the wrong time, and Cooper could be paralyzed. That meant he could no longer play the game he loved. The condition is not fatal, and Cooper Manning remains in good health today, but he couldn't step onto a football field again, unless he wanted to risk serious injury.

From that moment on, Cooper became a Peyton Manning fan. "I would like to live my dream of playing football through you," he wrote to his brother soon after his diagnosis.

Peyton was just fine with that, only he wasn't sure where that dream would happen. Although Cooper had followed his father's footsteps by attending the University of Mississippi, Peyton was attracting interest from schools all over the country. After Peyton threw for 2,345 yards (2,144 m) and 30 touchdowns his junior year at Newman High School, recruiting analysts rated him the top player in the country. It seemed as if everybody knew about him.

"He's got great athletic ability," said former Saints coach Jim Mora, who would later coach Peyton with the Colts. "If there's any better quarterback his age out there in the country, I'd just like to see him." The recruiting process was tough. Coaches called every night. University of Mississippi fans sent Peyton letters, encouraging him to follow in his father's footsteps and help revive the Rebels program. Reporters kept asking

> **"It was just like playing in the backyard."**
> **—Peyton Manning**

Boxes of Peyton Manning's recruiting letters.

questions. Everybody wanted to know the same thing: Where was Peyton going? Archie Manning wasn't about to influence his son to head to Ole Miss. He offered his advice and coached Peyton on how to handle the coaches and reporters. But he wasn't telling his son what to do.

"Some of my buddies have called and said, 'You make him go to Ole Miss,'" Archie Manning said. "They're real hardcore about it. And though I'm sure they mean well, they aren't thinking about what they'd do if Peyton was their son." Manning did what any good father would do. He let Peyton make his decision.

Peyton wasn't a naive high school senior. He knew all about the schools. He knew what kinds of offenses they ran. He knew their coaches and their traditions. If anybody was going to make an informed, intelligent decision in this situation, it was going to be Peyton. In the end, he chose the University of Tennessee. Then came the hate mail. And the nasty phone calls. To many Rebels fans, Peyton was a traitor. Meanwhile, Cooper walked around the Mississippi campus wearing a Tennessee Volunteers hat to show support for his brother's decision. It had been a tough process, but it was over. Peyton's chapter in Tennessee, however, was just beginning.

When Peyton Manning needs advice about football or life, he often turns to his father during a game of golf.

Peyton Manning enjoyed immediate success at Tennessee, taking over the starting quarterback job as a freshman.

CHAPTER THREE

Collegiate Hero

You couldn't blame Peyton Manning for being excited. Here he was, a raw college freshman, directing Tennessee's offense in a nationally televised game against the University of California at Los Angeles. The season wasn't even a game old and Peyton was in the eye of the storm. He buckled up his chinstrap and trotted out to the huddle.

"Okay," Peyton said. "We're going to go down the field and score a touchdown!"

The response was hardly overwhelming. "Shut up, rookie," one of the Volunteers linemen said. "Call the play."

The lineman's attitude didn't spoil Peyton's enthusiasm. When Tennessee Volunteer quarterbacks Jerry Colquitt and Todd Helton were injured early in the 1994 season, it was up to Peyton to fill the void. It wasn't going to be easy. Even though he had been a high school star and a big-time recruit, Peyton wasn't ready for college ball. No freshman quarterback is. But University of Tennessee coach Philip Fulmer knew he had a talented player and set about putting together a plan that would make the best use of his talents. The result was a simple offense that didn't ask Peyton to be too tricky or take too many risks.

Manning blossomed in the Tennessee offensive system, which helped him become a standout dropback passer.

"We were very cautious with him as a freshman," Fulmer said. "He had good players around him and he didn't have to win games for us by himself. We didn't want to destroy his confidence."

The results were largely positive. Tennessee finished the year with an 8 and 4 record, and Peyton threw for a respectable 1,141 yards (1,043 m) and 11 touchdowns. It was a strong debut, although it was not without its problems. Peyton completed just 5 of 22 passes against the University of Mississippi. He failed to spot a wide-open receiver in the last minute of the Volunteers' 17–13 loss to Alabama. When he failed to shine, Peyton heard the critics. Most wanted Tennessee to go with highly regarded freshman Branndon Stewart. But Peyton continued to work hard. He asked so many questions that some of the older players got annoyed. He practiced as hard as he played in games. He improved.

"He came in with an attitude that I've never seen in any freshman," former Volunteers running

"We were very cautious with him as a freshman. He had good players around him and he didn't have to win games for us by himself. We didn't want to destroy his confidence."
—Tennessee coach Philip Fulmer

back Eric Lane said. "He wanted to get as much work done as possible, every day." That attitude carried over into the summer. While some players took it easy, Peyton was organizing practices with his teammates.

"It was tough for me, adjusting to his work ethic," former Tennessee wide receiver Joey Kent said. "He was so young."

All the hard work paid off during the 1995 season. Tennessee finished 11 and 1 and Peyton threw for 2,954 yards (2,701 m) and 22 touchdowns. Perhaps more remarkable was his interception total: 4 in 380 pass attempts. He was particularly remarkable in a 49–31 win over Arkansas. Although the Razorbacks

Extra work and long hours were never a problem for Peyton.

University of Tennessee Football

Few schools in the country have a college football tradition as long and distinguished as does Tennessee. The school, based in Knoxville, has had outstanding teams, legendary coaches, and highly successful players.

The Volunteers (the name refers to the large number of Tennesseans who volunteered to join the American armies during the Revolutionary War and the War of 1812) may have lost their first-ever game, in 1891, to Sewanee (24–0). But they have tasted considerable success since. Tennessee entered the 2002 season with a combined record of 718–295–53 and ranks among the top ten in all-time wins. Tennessee has won two consensus national championships—in 1951 and 1988—and had four other teams (1938, 1940, 1950, and 1967) that received recognition by one or more organizations as the best team in the country.

How 'bout those Volunteers! Peyton celebrates another touchdown.

blitzed him every way possible throughout the afternoon, Peyton completed 35 of 46 passes for 384 yards (351 m) and 4 touchdowns. "We tried to make it complicated for him, and he handled everything," Arkansas defensive coordinator Joe Lee Dunn said. But it wasn't enough. It never is for Peyton. "He's like the coach's little son who's 5'9" and can't break an egg when he throws, except Peyton is 6'5" with a world of talent," Fulmer said.

In the spring following Peyton's sophomore year, professional scouts made their annual trip to Tennessee to get a look at the Volunteers' seniors-to-be. They asked Peyton about many of the players, and he asked them questions as well. He grilled one scout about defenses. He asked others about offenses. "After talking to him, it's obvious he's way ahead of most young quarterbacks," San Diego Chargers coach Dwain Painter said.

> **"He came in with an attitude that I've never seen in any freshman. He wanted to get as much work done as possible, every day."**
>
> **—Eric Lane**

Peyton's work on the field was impressive, but he was even more amazing when it came to watching film. All quarterbacks are expected to watch game tapes of their oppo-

By the time Saturday came, Manning had watched so much film of that week's Tennessee opponent that he was ready for anything.

nents, to learn about their defensive plays. Nobody watched more than Peyton. He would come back to his dorm room after practice and spend hours watching extra videos. His roommates called Peyton's room "the Cave," because he spent so much time in there alone. Peyton was so devoted to his homework that the Tennessee coaches had to prepare more.

David Cutcliffe, who was the Volunteers quarterback coach at that time, used to watch extra tape on Sundays because he knew Peyton would have plenty of questions at the team's Monday meeting. "He's somebody very special, and I don't want to let him down," Cutcliffe said.

Peyton certainly didn't let the Volunteers down in 1996. He threw for a school record: 3,287 yards (3,005 m) and 20 touchdowns. Tennessee went 10 and 2, and won the Citrus Bowl. It was obvious Peyton was a rare talent. And the NFL knew it.

"I didn't think there's ever been a quarterback who has been as prepared, mentally, as Manning is," one scout said.

"He's the first pick in the draft, last year, this year, next year, whenever he wants," another said.

Tennessee fans didn't like hearing that. They wanted Peyton to stay in school for his senior season. They dreamed that he would win the Heisman Trophy as the nation's best player and that he would lead the Volunteers to the national championship. It was decision time, and the spotlight was on Peyton. What would he do?

Peyton Manning ran the Tennessee offense with confidence and skill, using all of the weapons at his disposal.

CHAPTER FOUR

Decision Time

The choice, it seemed, was easy. Nearly everybody Peyton and his father spoke with said the same thing: it was time to move on to the NFL.

Peyton had done it all at Tennessee. Or just about all. He would graduate with a degree in speech communication and a 3.53 grade point average. He had passed for more than 7,000 yards (6,400 m) and 50 touchdowns. The NFL loved him. It was time to go. Three years in college was enough.

Although everybody expected Peyton to give up his senior season at Tennessee for NFL fame and fortune, the quarterback wasn't so sure. Even if nearly thirty players a year were leaving college early, he wasn't going to base his decision on what everybody else did. That wasn't his style.

Peyton went to work, just like always. He and his father talked to scouts, former players and coaches, current NFL stars, and other professional athletes. Dallas Cowboys quarterback Troy Aikman told Peyton he was ready for professional football. So did onetime New York Giants star Phil Simms. Even Tim Duncan, of the National Basketball Association's

Volunteers fans begged Peyton to return for his senior year at Tennessee.

San Antonio Spurs, advised Peyton to leave. Tennessee fans didn't know what information Peyton was receiving and they feared the worst.

In early March, when Peyton stepped up to the microphone at a jam-packed press conference, most Volunteers fans expected to hear him announce that he was leaving. Instead, they were given some great news. Peyton would be back at the University of Tennessee for his senior season. The NFL had always been his ultimate goal, but it could wait. "I'm entitled to play four years, so I'm going to," he said.

"I need to get into the NFL, I can't wait to get there, and I want that challenge. But I want it with every bit of ammunition I've got."
—Peyton Manning

The whole state celebrated. There were signs in almost every storefront window thanking him. His decision was a topic of discussion on a local news program. Everybody Peyton met congratulated him. He hadn't done what everyone else had. He had stayed—because he wanted to stay.

"I want to walk to class and hear people say, 'Good luck in the game,'" Peyton said. "I want to see that little orange section (of Tennessee fans) in the stands at road games. I really do. I want to tailgate with my parents after the games and then go out to dinner.

"What I did is selfish. I didn't do it because it's right for any other college athlete who has to make the same kind of decision. Michael Jordan, when I talked to him, told me to do what I want to do. That was the key word here: want. And, believe me, the decision was close."

Peyton enjoyed college football. There was no question about that. But he was also concerned that he might miss out on some vital preparation time by leaving early. For someone who always wanted to work harder than anyone else, that was important.

"I need to get into the NFL," Peyton said. "I can't wait to get there, and I want that challenge. But I want it with every bit of ammunition I've got."

At a press conference, Peyton Manning announces he will remain at Tennessee for his senior year.

Peyton was coming back. His return meant that Tennessee was a favorite to win the national championship. He was everybody's preseason choice to win the Heisman Trophy. He had the chance to break just about every passing record at Tennessee. But it wouldn't be easy. Tennessee was in the tough Southeastern Conference (SEC), and

Even though Peyton enjoyed considerable success at Tennessee, he was never able to beat arch-rival Florida.

that meant the Volunteers would play Florida every year. The Gators, under coach Steve Spurrier, had become the team to beat in the SEC, and a national powerhouse. They even won the 1996 national championship.

Peyton and the Volunteers had lost all three games he played against the Gators, including an ugly 62–37 decision his sophomore season. In 1997 it would be more of the same.

Peyton struggled against the fast Florida defense, and even threw an interception that was returned for a touchdown. The Gators beat the Volunteers, 33–20. It was a tough loss, but it was the only one Tennessee would suffer during the regular season. They captured the SEC title and won 11 games. Peyton threw for 3,819 yards (3,492 m) and 36 touchdowns, and was voted an All American.

> **"You can't overwork him. He's like a sponge. He wants to do the best he can, and he wants you to give him all that you can give him."**
>
> **—Colts coach Jim Mora**

The loss to Florida wasn't the only disappointment Peyton would face that year. When it came time for the Heisman balloting, voters chose Michigan defensive back Charles Woodson. Tennessee fans were furious. But Peyton congratulated Woodson, and chose not to criticize those who had voted him second. Besides, his college career was done. It was time to move on to the NFL.

As the NFL draft approached, there was another individual battle going on. This time, it was Peyton versus Ryan Leaf, a big, strong-armed quarterback from Washington State. Leaf had led the Cougars to the Pacific-10 Conference championship and the Rose Bowl, and was considered by some to be the best quarterback in the draft. Indianapolis held the first pick, and everybody wanted to know who the Indianapolis Colts would choose. Some believed it would be Peyton, thanks to his great four-year career, sharp mind, great work ethic, and overwhelming skill. Those who favored Leaf liked his powerful arm and strong physique. Peyton or Ryan?

On draft day, Indianapolis put all the questions to rest by making Peyton the first pick. The Colts were thrilled to have him and predicted Peyton would help them improve on their 3 and 13 record in 1997.

"He's the kind of guy who wants to be coached," former Colts head coach Jim Mora said. "You can't overwork him. He's like a sponge. He wants to do the best he can, and he wants you to give him all that you can give him."

Peyton was about to get it, NFL style.

It was smiles all around when Indianapolis made Peyton Manning the top pick in the 1998 NFL draft.

NFL life is unpredictable, so Manning is ready for anything—even the occasional scramble from the pocket.

CHAPTER FIVE

The Professional Life

It all came together in three minutes. The Colts were down 6 points, with the ball on their own 20-yard line against the Jets. Peyton Manning was eleven weeks into his 1998 rookie year in Indianapolis, and it was time to show the world what he had learned.

It had been a rough debut for the heralded rookie. In his first nine games, Manning had thrown 12 touchdown passes but had been intercepted 18 times. The Colts' offense had struggled, averaging just 16 points.

"I forced a number of throws," Manning said. "And, sure, you might say 'rookie mistakes,' but pretty much just dumb quarterback mistakes are what I called them."

Manning looked pretty smart in those final minutes against the New York Jets. He led the Colts down the field for the game-winning touchdown. The rest of the season was more of the same. Even though Indianapolis finished just 3 and 13, Manning proved he could quarterback in the NFL. Over the last seven games, he had 14 touchdowns and 10 interceptions. It was almost like he had crammed two seasons into one.

"There was an unbelievable difference from the first eight games to the second eight games," Colts quarterback coach Bruce Arias said.

Peyton Manning reaches to hand off the ball to a teammate.

Manning set an NFL rookie record by throwing 575 passes. He also established rookie marks with 3,739 yards (3,419 m) and 26 touchdowns. All those people who had wondered whether the Colts had chosen the right quarterback were not wondering anymore. Peyton Manning was thriving in Indianapolis.

The Colts knew that they had done the right thing almost from the start. Not only had Manning impressed them before the draft, but he continued to impress them after it, too.

Manning takes a moment to talk to the Colts offensive coordinator, Tom Moore.

Manning took part in a three-day mini-practice session in May 1998 before returning home for a month. While there, he watched game tapes, studied the *playbook,* and called Colts coaches with questions.

When he returned for training camp, he was clearly prepared for action. "It was very obvious he had done his homework," then Colts head coach Jim Mora said. "He made considerable improvement; you could tell he had done a lot of work. He came back with an overall understanding of our offense."

That was no small accomplishment. Manning had to know how to change plays at the *line of scrimmage* if he had to. He had to learn about Indianapolis's seventeen different pass-protection schemes. The coaches kept asking questions and Peyton kept giving answers. Right answers.

"Nobody watches more tape than Peyton," said Dom Anile, the Colts' director of football operations. "He could study film until the cows come home. If it's a coverage [play] that's been used somehow, somewhere in our league, he [has] seen it, and he understands it, and I guarantee he knows how to attack it."

When Manning began his second season with the Colts, he was almost like a veteran.

There are few more dangerous passing combinations than Peyton to Marvin Harrison. Here, they celebrate a touchdown.

But he didn't act like one. He still seemed to work harder than anybody else on the team. By the time his second year began, Manning was more vocal, too. That's not always the easiest thing to do. Football players aren't just given respect. They have to earn it.

"It's his huddle, and he'll tell you that," Colts guard Adam Meadows said. "So when he's talking, everybody is listening. You can't say a word."

Critics were silenced by the end of year two also. How could they complain? Manning

"He could study film until the cows come home. If it's a coverage [play] that's been used somehow, somewhere in our league, he [has] seen it, and he understands it, and I guarantee he knows how to attack it."
— Dom Anile

completed 62 percent of his passes for 4,135 yards (3,781 m) and 26 touchdowns. His interception total dropped from 28 his rookie year to 15. Peyton was more decisive and efficient than he had been as a rookie. It was a great performance, one that earned Manning his first Pro Bowl invitation.

More importantly, the Colts won the American Football Conference East Division title with a 13 and 3 record and advanced to the play-offs. Though they lost to Tennessee, 19–16, in the divisional play-offs, it was a good first step for Manning. And things were going to get even better.

Peyton on the move!

There can be no question of who is in charge of the Colts' offense. It's Peyton Manning.

CHAPTER SIX

Stardom Beckons

On November 11, 2001, Peyton Manning broke his jaw in a game against Miami at the RCA Dome. Many believed the durable quarterback was headed for the bench. Indeed, backup Mark Rypien did finish the game. It was an injury that had sent other men to the sidelines for three or four weeks. But the next week, Peyton Manning was back. He might not have been able to eat a steak, but he was okay to play in New Orleans. By the time the 2001 season was over, Manning had started sixty-four consecutive games for the Colts. He had been with the team four years, and his leadership, which had blossomed during his second season, was now unquestioned. Football is about playing with pain, and Manning had proved himself by buckling his chinstrap over a broken jaw.

When the Colts went 6 and 10 and missed out on the play-offs after two years in the postseason, he was angry. He didn't care about how impressive his numbers were. He cared about winning. That much was evident in the winter of 2002 when the Colts named former Tampa Bay coach Tony Dungy as their new boss. It didn't take long for Dungy to see how valuable Manning was to the team. After spending six weeks watching film of the Colts, Dungy knew what NFL fans had known for years. The team's future is Peyton Manning.

A job well done: former Colts coach Jim Mora congratulates Peyton after another touchdown pass.

After leading the Colts to the play-offs in 1999, Manning had quite an encore the next year. He set club records and led the NFL with 4,413 passing yards (4,035 m) and 33 touchdowns. Manning passed for more than 300 yards (274 m) in five different games, with a 440-yard (402-m) 4-touchdown show against Jacksonville. Manning led the Colts to wins in their last three games to clinch a wild card play-off spot against the Dolphins. Even though Indianapolis lost a heartbreaker to Miami when a late field-goal try by Mike Vanderjagt failed, it was still a great year. The NFL rewarded Peyton with a second straight invitation to the Pro Bowl in Hawaii.

After just three years in the league, Manning was clearly a rising star. Some might have said he had already reached the top. "He has a chance to be one of the best ever," Colts offensive coordinator Tom Moore said. "He has the ability. He has the smarts, and he has the great work ethic. He's just a tireless worker."

Much of the credit for the Colts' success goes to Manning, but running back Edgerrin James (32) is also one of the league's best.

As the 2001 season dawned, many felt the Colts were getting close to becoming true Super Bowl contenders. They certainly had the offense for it. In Manning, running back Edgerrin James, and wide receiver Marvin Harrison, Indianapolis had three lethal weapons. In 2000 Manning and James became the first *tandem* from the same team to lead the NFL in passing and *rushing* yards.

In addition to being a leader on the field, Peyton Manning always makes time to reach out to his younger fans.

The 2001 season promised to be an exciting one, especially when Indianapolis began by winning its first two games. But the Colts stumbled after that, losing three in a row. After two more wins, the Colts dropped five straight. Then, James suffered a knee injury that knocked him out for the rest of the season. Indianapolis fell from play-off contention,

Football can be very rough. Here, Peyton Manning is taken down by two Oakland Raiders.

and that caused some trouble within the team. Former Colts coach Jim Mora even publicly questioned Manning's play after a late-December 40–21 home loss to San Francisco. In the game, Manning threw 4 interceptions. One was returned for a touchdown, the fifth time that had happened that year.

"Do not blame that game on the defense," Mora said after the game. "I don't care who you play, a high school team, a junior college team, a college team . . . when you turn the ball over five times, you ain't going to beat anybody. That was a disgraceful performance."

Manning was stung by Mora's comments. He had never been publicly criticized like that before. Here he was, playing with his jaw partially wired shut, without his best running back, and he was being scolded. To his credit, Manning did not shout back at the coach, choosing to talk privately with Mora. When the year

Peyton Manning is sacked in a play against the Baltimore Ravens in 2001.

was over, and the memories of the 6 and 10 season had begun to fade, Manning could reflect on another fine season. He had thrown for 4,131 yards (3,777 m) and 26 scores. He had become the only player in NFL history to throw for more than 3,000 yards (2,743 m) in each of his first four seasons. He was just the fifth player ever to have three years with more than 4,000 passing yards (3,657 m).

As the Tony Dungy era began in Indianapolis, the new coach knew the Colts needed to improve their defense. He knew the Colts needed a healthy Edgerrin James carrying the ball. He also knew that the quarterback position was as secure as any in the NFL.

"I've been impressed," Dungy said. "[Peyton's] very talented, watching him on tape. I think he wants to continue to improve. Winning and improving are very

Peyton Manning calls a play in a game against the Philadelphia Eagles in 2002.

important to him. With a guy like Peyton, you're just happy you've got him, and you know he's going to continue to work and get better at it."

There's no question about that. Peyton Manning is a star now, but because of his commitment and willingness to work hard, he'll accomplish even more.

Stats

Stats

Peyton Manning

Born: March 25, 1976

College: Tennessee

Years in the NFL: 5

Team: Indianapolis Colts

Team #: 18

Height: 6' 5"

Weight: 220 lbs. (100 kg)

Year	Games	Games Started	Attempted Passes	Completed Passes	%	Yards	Yards per attempt	Longest	Touchdown	Interceptions	Rate
1998	16	16	575	326	56.7	3,739	6.5	78td	26	28	71.2
1999	16	16	533	331	62.1	4,135	7.8	80dt	26	15	90.7
2000	16	16	571	357	62.5	4,413	7.7	78td	33	15	94.7
2001	16	16	547	343	62.7	4,131	7.6	86td	26	23	84.1
2002	16	16	591	392	66.3	4,200	7.1	69	27	19	88.8
Total	80	80	2,817	1,749	62.1	20,618	7.3	86td	138	100	85.9

Rushing

Year	Games	Games Started	Attempted Passes	Yards	Average	Touchdowns
1998	16	16	15	62	4.1	0
1999	16	16	35	73	2.1	2
2000	16	16	37	116	3.1	1
2001	16	16	35	157	4.5	4
2002	16	16	38	148	3.9	2
Total	80	80	160	556	3.5	9

Figures compiled from NFL.com.

GLOSSARY

blitz—A rush of the passer by the defense that includes more players than just the defensive linemen, a team's traditional pass rushers. This can include one extra player, or up to four or five additional defenders.

down—One of four consecutive plays in which a team, in order to keep possession of the ball, must either score or advance the ball 10 yards for a first down and another set of four downs.

fake—To deceive. A quarterback will often fake handing the ball to a running back in order to fool the defense into thinking that it must defend against a running play. The quarterback will then look to pass the ball.

Heisman Trophy—The award given annually to the best player in college football. It was first given in 1936.

playbook—A collection of a team's strategies and schemes, issued each season to players who are expected to memorize it and keep it secret from all people outside the team.

Pro Bowl—The annual game, played in Honolulu, pitting the best players from the National Football Conference (NFC) against the best from the American Football Conference (AFC).

quarterback—The offensive back who calls the signals, directs the plays, and throws the passes for a team.

rushing—The act of running the ball upfield by an offensive back. Also refers to the act of a defensive player's attempt to reach the quarterback by eluding or overpowering offensive linemen.

scrimmage—The play that follows the pass from the center to the quarterback. Line of scrimmage: the part of the field from which a play begins.

snap—The act of passing the ball from the center to the quarterback.

tandem—A cooperation and mutual dependence between two players.

touchdown—A scoring play, worth 6 points, in which a player brings the ball across the opponent's goal line.

FIND OUT MORE

Web Sites

NFL Official Site
NFL.com

Sports Illustrated for Kids NFL Player Pages
http://www.sikids.com/news/nflplayer/index.html

Peyton Manning Official Web Site
www.peytonmanning.com

Books

Buckley, James Jr. *Peyton Manning*. New York: DK Publishing, 2001.

Hymans, Jimmy. *Peyton Manning: Primed and Ready*. Lenexa, KS: Addax Publishing Group, 1998.

National Football League. *Official NFL 2002 Record and Fact Book*. New York: Workman Publishing, 2000.

Savage, Jeff. *Peyton Manning: Precision Passer*. Minneapolis, MN: Lerner Publications Co., 2001.

Stewart, Mark. *Peyton Manning: Rising Son*. Brookfield, CT: Millbrook Press, 2000.

The Ultimate NFL Quarterback Club Sticker Book. New York: DK Publishing, 2002.

INDEX

Page numbers in **boldface** are illustrations.